ESSAYS ON M

❧

Essays on Marriage

Seikan Hasegawa

GREAT OCEAN PUBLISHERS
ATLANTA, GEORGIA

Essays on Marriage is the second in a series of books by Seikan Hasegawa to be published by Great Ocean Publishers. The first book in the series is *The Cave of Poison Grass, Essays on the Hannya Sutra*, the third *Mind to Mind*. The books deal with various subjects, but their common theme and purpose is that of Zen training: the practical study of how to live best in each and every situation. The series is entitled COMPANIONS OF ZEN TRAINING.

Copyright © 1999 by Seikan Hasegawa
Front cover illustration copyright © 1977 by Seikan Hasegawa
Back cover and text illustrations copyright © 1999 by Taiyo Hasegawa

For further information contact:

Great Ocean Publishers
1788 Queens Way
Atlanta, Georgia 30341

Second edition

Library of Congress Cataloging in Publication Data

Hasegawa, Seikan, 1945 –
  Essays on Marriage / Seikan Hasegawa. — 2nd ed.
    p. cm. — (Companions of Zen training)
    ISBN 0-915556-36-7 (alk. paper)
    1. Marriage   I. Title. II. Series: Hasegawa, Seikan, 1945–
  Companions of Zen training
  HQ734.H366   1999   99-25879
  306.81—DC21   CIP

Printed in the United States of America   10 9 8 7 6 5 4 3 2 1

Contents

Choosing a Marriage Partner

We wish to choose the most suitable partner for our marriage. However, it is evident that we are greatly limited in searching for a partner no matter how much time and energy we spend at it. There are limits in two directions: the knowledge we have of others and the knowledge we have of ourselves.

To choose the most suitable partner, we would have to be able to obtain every bit of necessary information about people, especially of the opposite sex. Without understanding all people of the opposite sex we cannot choose anyone as our marriage partner; there are too many people in too many places. It is absurd if someone thinks he or she has chosen the best partner on this earth. Without even so much as glancing at everyone of the opposite sex, how can one choose one's best partner? He and she may say they did their best. But their best is almost meaningless because it is too tiny to be a real best, and rather harmful because they may take some pride in their tiny best.

There are too many people for us to understand if we want to choose our best marriage partner. Yet with the desire to choose the best partner, and with the illusion that we can, we set out on our search. And if we have some experiences with twenty or thirty or at the most three hundred of the opposite sex, what can we understand? Losing virginity, losing time to concentrate on our love for one person, we gain nothing but guilt, self-hatred, and old age. We are better off knowing that we have no ability to choose our best marriage partner.

Nowadays we are benefited by a comparatively freer world. In past centuries we had no effective transportation and means of communicating; moreover, we had blind boundaries of race and society. So we hardly had the freedom to choose our partner as we wished. Things are certainly getting better, but when we see the fact that we cannot meet with everyone on earth even if we use the tools of the highest scientific attainment such as airplanes, computers, televisions, and artificial satellites, we cannot say that our freedom to search out a partner has been greatly widened. Our capacity to choose our best partner is disappointingly limited. Someday our descendants will enjoy the freedom to meet anyone without spending much time and energy, but will they be any more able to choose their best partner?

To choose our best partner we would have to know not only who other people are, but also who we are. Without knowing what kind of partner we want to have, we cannot choose anyone. Frankly, we don't know who we are, and naturally we aren't sure what kind of person we want to have. The person who thinks he is sure of what kind of human being he is and what kind of partner he wants is the person who knows himself least. No matter how steady a view he has, such a steady view will change when the situation in which he lives changes. "Swear not at all; neither by the heaven, nor by the earth, nor by thy head for thou canst not stop their changing even a moment." Every form changes. It is a dangerous thing to marry with a particular, fixed affection for one's partner because it will change sooner or later. People cannot know who they are unless they go through religious training and enlighten themselves. So, people are limited in choosing their best partner because they themselves don't know what kind of partner they want.

Someday we will know more about ourselves and we will be sure of how we should live. If such a time comes, will we be sure of what kind of partner we want to have?

To spend much energy and time choosing our marriage partner is therefore a silly thing. It is evident that no matter how much of our energy and time we spend choosing, we cannot find our best partner.

The best thing we can do is spend the least energy and time choosing our marriage partner and spend the most energy and time building up our married life. To marry is not as important as to live married life.

Despite our limitations and the limits of our situation, people are still choosing. This is because they don't realize that choosing is a disrespectful act for reverend human beings who do not like to be unfair. We can choose only when we compare two or more persons in front of us and give them each a different value. It is true that all people are different physically and mentally. Seeing people's differences is pure wisdom, but placing value on these differences is the result of our egoistic estimation. We cannot give a fair estimate, because our ego is made out of our uncertain relativity. Should we judge a person only from our standpoint? Each person has a different situation, education, position, nationality, etc. Being chosen or being compared with others by a person with decided taste and prejudice isn't an enjoyable matter. "Say, your vagina is better than X's." Choosing a marriage partner in this way is not admirable, and enjoying being chosen is sadly stupid. The person who is chosen for marriage by a comparison with others is fated to be rejected later by similar comparison. A reverend human being shouldn't choose a person and shouldn't be chosen.

If we so enjoy choosing and being chosen, we have to give the same right and ability to our babies who will be born. Babies with their imperfect knowledge don't choose us. If we are going to choose a certain type of child, we will make a dark problem for all of us.

If we have to choose a partner for married life, we should choose without making any comparisons.

How can we choose a partner without comparing him or her with others? We can do so by chance. And if we make sure of only one thing, we can marry without spending a lot of time and energy, and without living a dishonorable life. This one thing we have to make sure of is loyalty to each other. Loyalty is enough to make a worthy and enjoyable married life. But without loyalty, any other virtues aren't enough for success in making a happy married life.

What is loyalty? Loyalty is the life of marriage. Without loyalty no one can marry, and we had better not live such a married life. Loyalty has three basic aspects: a great wish to live a worthy married life, an indomitable determination to attain a worthy married life, and an unfading belief that such a worthy married life can be attained. If there is this loyalty, people will know what love is.

Virginity

One winter afternoon I was watching quietly through a window, expecting snow to begin falling. The sun was completely hidden by the silent but steadily passing clouds. The leafless trees dared not move. I knew that each snowflake had its individual movement in the air as if it were a living creature, and yet I couldn't free myself from worrying that it would stop falling and the sun shine an unnecessary smile. When each snowflake lost its individual character and became a mere element of the senseless stream of snow from sky to ground, I began to say to myself, "Nice, nice, it is snowing, certainly it is snowing!" My mother used to come behind me at such a moment and say to me, "Tomorrow morning you will see a pure white world, the world of Buddha. Now pull the curtain and come to supper."

Next morning, just as I had hoped, I could see a vast white world in front of my eyes, the clean, pure, gentle, rhythmical world of snow with nothing invading its serene beauty. I went out and walked on the snow, careful to disturb it as little as possible with my footprints, and proceeded to the center of the snow world, across the fields, through the forest keeping its sincere quiet. I didn't stride around kicking the snow to scatter it into the air, leaving an ugly trace of violence, nor shake the snowy tree branches and raise a temporarily exciting noise. I walked quietly, enjoying the feeling that I was in the world of snow, and I sought the pleasure of entering into its center, hoping to become snow if I could. How disappointed I felt when I saw five or six children of my age jumping around with their dogs and sleds and throwing snowballs at one another. I turned my back to them and went to the more remote part of my village.

Most children don't realize the enjoyment of being part of greater and more beautiful things but only know the enjoyment of separating from them and fighting against them. Naturally most adults have to experience the bitterness of self-pity and self-hatred, because as long as our brain is functioning correctly, we must face the fact that no matter how much we try to separate from things greater than us, or try to conquer them, still we are mere humble, mortal, imperfect, ghostly beings. In trying to be independent of the world, nature, or the universe, we will find only that we have lost even the meaning of why we are living and the cause of how we are now thus living. The enjoyment of being a part of greater things, of trying to be unified with things more beautiful than us, is what enables us to find the meaning and the cause of our life and to appreciate our life. While our sense organs are attracted by the surface of colors and forms, we may not notice that our basic desire is to be unified with eternal, absolute, and perfect being. However, the person who begins to think about the meaning and the cause of all sorts of phenomena in this world, who isn't satisfied to spend his life moment after moment only with impulsive thoughts, forced to do so by his surroundings, the person who likes to be a specialist at least about his own life, hating not to know even what his life is, will realize that we basically want to live in eternal, universal life.

When we think about virginity, if we discuss whether it is right or wrong without awareness of our basic desire to be unified with greater being, our discussion will become wasteful babble, both pitiful and comical, like fish flapping on the shore.

It must be fun for young couples to undress and touch each other's secret parts. Seeing only each other's surface doesn't give enough enjoyment since faces are much too made up. A great part of our culture is maintaining its order by unreal ideas and forms. One can hardly see an un-phony human. On every occasion young people wish to see a real face that doesn't lie. On a beach with a pine forest, at the foot of a mountain with a stream, regardless of place, even in a sweet potato field, even in an airplane toilet, young people want to see a real face of the opposite sex, especially of a person who has some possibility of being frank and kind, and of being respected. They want to make sure of what it means when the opposite sex says "yes," or "no," make sure of the real meaning of his or her laugh or cry. If young people see the possibility of giving enjoyment to each other and taking away suffering from each other, it means they want to see the harmony of the two contradictory sexes. People know harmony is one of the most important elements for our happiness, and they know instinctively that harmony can be realized when a contradiction unifies itself. After all, our life is the result of a harmony and our form is eagerly seeking the harmony of its own contradictory character. Fortunately young people have enough energy to seek this harmony, and enough enjoyment will arise when they are seeking it. So having sex is not only fun, pleasurable, and enjoyable, but also bright, wonderful, and constructive.

However, virginity is a problem for people who love our life and reflect upon themselves to find out the best way to live.

What is virginity? Virginity is to keep one's body untouched sexually before marriage so as to use it as a proof of trust, respect, and love for one's partner in marriage. This means virginity consists of two aspects. One is physical, which is "body untouched sexually." The other is mental, which is "so as to use it as a proof of trust, respect, and love." Neither of these two aspects without the other can define virginity. Look at a three-year-old girl. She has no will to be a virgin, so as to this consideration she is just a pee kid. Or imagine a spiritual Peter Pan who carries hay to his cows all day long, thinking only of apple cider and blankets. He and virginity have less relation than milk and a fisherman's net. On the other hand, it is clear that

even if a person expresses his great love with the eloquence of Goethe or Picasso, he cannot be a virgin for his second or third marriage. So everyone has the possibility of being a virgin, though it has no function in itself unless the purpose of being a virgin is realized.

Virginity has been such an important concern for most people since old times because of its mysterious beauty. One aspect of virginity comes naturally from our being born into this world, and the other comes from the human, deep wish to live well. That is to say, virginity is a flower raised by nature and human beings. This flower, virginity, is great beauty. It is the most suitable flower to decorate the entrance of the world of trust, respect, and love.

Nature gave us rain, snow, rivers, mountains, fields, and all other numerous things. All the things nature gives us are beautiful, but given only once. The things nature gives us are never repeated and as long as we live we can enjoy them each only once. Think about a mountain given by nature. If we once destroy it, when can we see the same mountain again? Once we pollute the ocean, how can we expect to see the original ocean? Nature changes without stopping and never repeats. For dull eyes, which cannot distinguish even sugar from salt, which can see no difference between cheese and soap, nature seems the same. Yesterday was the same as today, tomorrow will be no different from today, because for a person with dull eyes the same sun rises and sets. But the fact is that things of nature come only once for us. Virginity is also given to us by nature only once and can never come again.

When I was a child I loved to be in a snowy field standing quietly, taking care not to disturb the world of snow with my thoughtless movement. I wanted to be a part of the snow world if I could. Growing up, I still had the desire to be a part of virginity; is it only my special desire? If people can understand the beauty of a snow world, can't they see more beauty in the virginity given half by nature? Can't people see the greatness of such nature, which produced the possibility of virginity? No one can gain virginity by his or her wish alone, without the power of nature, but everyone can perfect virginity by the wish to trust, respect, and love his or her marriage partner.

How can we complete the virginity given by nature?

Nature gave us only one aspect of virginity. Now we must perfect it with our earnest wish to use it for the person whom we can trust, respect, and love, and from whom these things can be received. My hope for young people is that they will have a strong and continuous wish to find such a person, to be found by such a person. Living with such a strong wish is the life of virginity. Enjoy the life of virginity until such a suitable marriage partner is found. Find such a suitable marriage partner and see each other's virginity. In such a wedding each will see nature through the other's virginity and will see humanity through the other's virginity. That is the time one begins to live real married life.

It is sad to see many young people who never realize the great beauty of virginity, who, while they are not realizing it, trample down the possibility of being virgins. Because of their ignorance, most people were never virgins. And they marry. What is their marriage? If marriage has any relation with nature and humanity, shouldn't we think that without virginity it is hard to succeed at living a great, beautiful, and enjoyable married life?

There is no use crying after the boat has set sail for the other shore. There is nothing better than taking care about two things. One is to think, "Then what is the best thing for me to do from now on?" And two, "How can I use my experience for younger people?"

Observe deeply, think well about nature and our life. Nothing is an unrelated matter for religious training, and virginity is no exception.

For Those Who Are Not Virgins

In this age there are many people who happen to lose their virginity with others rather than with the very partner they are going to marry. Virginity has consequently come to be held in lower regard than other virtues, or there are instances of its deterioration regardless of a clear order of values.

Virginity is respectable, but here it will be said that even people who lose their virginity with others before they marry can live a happy and excellent married life.

There are all sorts of people. There may be some people who are glad of having had the experience of losing their virginity with others before they marry. There may be some who even look back on it with pride, and also there are those who have mixed feelings and thoughts. In any case, it is natural and unavoidable to look back on our past acts with some reflection and examination.

An important attitude is to fully use our ability to look back and gain a good effect for the present and future of our marriage. In other words, we must learn from our past. It is wasteful if we treat our own past like those classics stashed away in libraries, as we often see, rarely read.

There is no worse treatment of our past than to disregard it and neglect it. The experience of losing virginity is one of our own classics worthy of being read often, from time to time, for the sake of our married life now and in the future. If possible, it is recommendable that marriage partners be generous enough with each other and earnest enough students to begin their marriage by reading and investigating their own classics.

However, such work isn't an easy task for people who can only remember the experience of losing their virginity with a sense of pain or denial — in short, with regret. For such people, such work is an unwelcome severity unless they are met with deep sympathy, sensitive comfort, and bright encouragement, and more, unless they come to realize the great meaning in doing so.

As to this point, we have to be aware that we have something that forms the nucleus of our privacy, related not only to the loss of virginity but to all sorts of matters. This is a problem we have to face before we can learn from the past. No matter how much we know that learning from the past is recommendable, if the past is unpleasant even to be remembered, we prefer to bury it in the dust, out of reach of people's eyes, even more than any classics buried in a library. We wish it to be concealed even from our own eyes, not to mention the eyes of others.

The present of a human being is nothing other than an extension of the past, yet the present isn't exactly the past by any means. The past threatens the present, and the future tends to be beyond our concern.

But because the present is a continuation of the past, the past occasionally surfaces against our wish. We then try to put it down, to ignore it. An unpleasant past is hard to treat, it is dark with no light really provided, and messy from not being kept in order. And such a past is forming our present complicated character.

Our past is the base of our character, and this character is what distinguishes us from others. Without it there wouldn't be each of us as we presently are.

This is the reason why by all means we must study our own past and our partner's past in order to love deeply and to know each other well in our married life. If we can learn from our past, our learning will complete our married life now and in the future. At the same time it will fulfill one of the ways of learning about human beings.

We had better not hurry but take time, be patient, spend months and years to look at our own past and learn about each other's past while respecting and loving each other.

The experience of losing virginity is beneficial for us as marriage partners as long as it is given life as our dear classic. This classic, which is the experience of losing virginity, is a fountain of love and wisdom if it is read with respect, and it could be a source of gloomy ignorance and distrust if it is not read at all.

Marriage Quarrels

A husband and a wife are fighting animals. No matter how deeply they trust, respect, and love each other in the depths of their hearts, they cannot avoid quarreling occasionally during a long married life since each is different from the other and each loves his or her own difference.

All phenomena, whether spiritual, mental, or physical, are different from one another. No two things are the same. A husband and a wife are not only no exception to this; it is also one reason why they marry. As long as marriage partners see the difference between themselves they have to fight, because they have different interests, demands, and views. But when they fight they forget their sameness, which was another reason why they married. Therefore if they can see sameness when difference arises with its cause for fighting, then they can respect each other. And if they can see difference when sameness arises too much, then each has no reason to feel the other is disgusting but can feel deeply rooted love. Trust will be built up by such a couple over the years.

However, reality for us is not so simple and poetical. Few people are wise enough not to fight. Most people have no such calm, surplus power. Rather, their brains are busily occupied in expressing their own viewpoint instead of being concerned with their partner's situation. Asserting our ego is one of our pleasures. Even if we know in a corner of our brain that by asserting our ego we are harming another who is a beloved wife or husband, still we cannot resist the pleasure of insisting and even the pleasure of seeing the opponent getting harmed. Even while knowing that harming others makes us regretful and increases our wrinkles, still we go on harming as if we were devils for others and for ourselves. I believe that in married life almost no one quarrels without knowing it is causing them suffering. No one wants to fight once they have loved, shared their bed, even had their children. Then why should they fight?

One of the earliest questions I had in my life was why loving persons must fight. Seeing my parents fighting, I asked myself this question as often as it rains. I could find a reason why strangers fight. They fight, I thought, because they don't love each other but feel like enemies. But it wasn't easy to rationalize why my parents, a wife and a husband, should fight. 'If they must fight, why should they stay together?' I asked myself. 'If they must fight, why did they create many children? They must be loving each other, after all,' I thought in my confusion.

It was a New Year's day when I was nine or ten. Because it was the biggest holiday for us, my senior sister and two senior brothers returned to their native house with nice presents from the towns where they worked. My junior sister and I were happy and cheerful and we visited the house of one of our school friends in the evening. There children of our village gathered together, had supper, played many games, and sang as many songs as we knew. Knowing our sister and brothers were home with presents, my junior sister and I were enraptured. My sister, so carried away by the occasion, was outspoken about the taste of the refreshments. "There's not enough sugar in this," she said, and all the other children burst into laughter.

Even amidst the high noise of kids' excitement we could clearly hear a certain exclamation from outside our friend's house. I was the first to make sense of the cry and I jumped up and ran from the house. My sister ran after me. Instinctively I could tell that my mother and father had begun to quarrel and that my mother was escaping from the beast's hand of my father. 'See! I couldn't believe spending such a happy time,' I said in my mind.

Outside was dark and it had begun to sleet. On a small wooden bridge I found my mother, kneeling and trembling. "Where are my brothers?" I asked her.

"They escaped to the mountain, they climbed to the top, I hope," my mother said.

"Where did my sister go?"

"I'm not sure, we ran together into the bamboo grove and separated. I hope, hope she wasn't caught."

"Soon my father will come here to find us, we must go somewhere else," I said. Just then there was the sound of someone pushing their way through the grasses by the riverside.

"Mama, Mama." It was my senior sister. Before her white face appeared out of the dark we felt the earth shake. It was my father's thudding pursuit of my mother.

"You go with her," I pushed my junior sister who was clinging to my elbow. She ran after our senior sister and disappeared into the darkness.

"Now we must go," I said, and my mother and I went down the bank through the dried eulalia. We walked along the river and occasionally stopped to listen for the sound of my father. My father's shouts reached our ears like thunder from a far-off place.

"Where are you?" "I'll kill you!" "Idiot!" . . .

We got soaking wet from the sleet, and sometimes we fell

into the water, slipping down from the pathless eulalia bank. My mother walked and chanted, "My children, please be safe, escape to a safe place, don't get caught." It was growing late, probably after ten at night. I imagined the faces of my playmates, 'What did they see and what are they feeling?'

I had a flashlight but didn't use it, because we would show my mad father where we were. We arrived beneath a big bridge and rested there.

"I will go to the police to report your father, please come with me," my mother urged me.

"Report him? . . . Probably that's the best we can do now," I said and we climbed up from beneath the bridge. Now we could walk on the road. It was fortunate that we were not visible in the dark night and our footsteps could not be heard in the falling sleet.

In the neighboring village there was a police cottage. There a policeman and his family were enjoying the New Year's holiday. We entered the residential area and walked soundlessly along the street. Even though by now it was midnight, some houses had bright lights with people happily celebrating the New Year. I could see the setting in my mind, hearing high excited chatter and laughter coming out through the windows.

In front of the police cottage we stood and hesitated to enter. 'Shameful! asking such a thing of the policeman as his first work in this new year,' I read my mother's heart. 'But I must report my husband, now.'

Finally she knocked on the door and said, "Excuse me for bothering you in this late night." The response from within was slow in coming. 'Inside the police cottage the family is going to bed after a happy holiday,' we thought. The policeman opened the door for us. He didn't show an unpleasant face, but it was evident that he was enjoying drinking wine. He quickly turned up the fire in his office stove and gave me a towel to wipe my wet hair. He understood the case well because he knew my family. To my mother he showed his sympathy, but then he turned his chair toward me and put his big hands heavily on my shoulders and gazed at me.

"Hey, how old are you, eight or nine? You must be suffering, eh? But don't be defeated by such a tiny suffering. You are a boy. A boy should be strong and find the correct way for his own life."

I kept silent. My mother was sobbing beside me. "Now I ask, not your mother, but you directly. Listen, I can arrest your father and put him in jail immediately if you want me to. But think a moment. If you say yes, you'll be the child of a criminal forever. Your mother may divorce him and you will always be a child without a father. Do you want to be that way all your life? If not, then even amid the torture of marriage quarrels, even in the sleet of night, be patient. Have the courage to live brightly and wait for the time when still having both your parents you can attain enough power to live your own healthy life in society. Tell me, which is better, putting handcuffs on your father or living with him even if he is crazy?"

I lost the ability to think, under his heavy hands. But finally I said, "My father isn't only bad, he is also good. The situation makes him bad sometimes, and makes him good sometimes."

The policeman released me and preached to my mother and encouraged her with a thousand words. I mostly don't remember what he said because I wasn't hearing.

It was very late, maybe early morning. We left. The sleet had stopped and there were stars. We felt very cold and tried to find some shed in which to spend the rest of the night. We knew we couldn't go home, because of my father. We found a straw hutch and fell asleep in the pile of straw. My mother was worrying about her other children and prayed for their safety.

This is only one of a million examples of how children suffer from marriage quarrels. Not only the people who fight suffer.

When we see the fighting between a husband and wife subjectively, such a marriage quarrel is surely one of our greatest sufferings. It instantly has a severe and fatal effect on the happiness of the individuals directly involved. But in many cases if a husband and wife don't fight, they can maintain their pleasure in life even if their country is becoming sick from its fighting, pollution, economic crises, and so on.

If we don't fight in our married life, we can lessen the suffering that occurs in our society and country. Moreover, we can contribute through our happy married life to building a healthy society and a peaceful world. If we fight, the suffering of society and the world increases ten times, a hundred times, and that suffering will return to us in a vicious circle, amplified.

We must try to solve our marriage quarrels, must make an effort to maintain a happy married life with the pride of thinking that world peace comes out of our married life.

How can we stop fighting with each other, how can we spend our happy, worthy married life without quarrels? Are we fighting animals? Yes, we are. However, we are also human beings, and if we truly become human beings, there is the way to fight and not to fight. If we become real human beings, we don't mind whether we fight or not.

Jealousy

No one can quarrel without an opponent. Any kind of marriage quarrel is no exception. Certainly where there is a marriage quarrel the cause is in both partners. However, when the cause of a marriage quarrel is related to jealousy, people have to be very thoughtful as well as warmly sympathetic before they conclude, "It takes two to make a quarrel."

In any case, one can feel jealous only when one loves one's partner. Jealousy without love is like smoke without fire. Naturally, when the feeling of jealousy isn't correctly resolved, it turns to hate. So, since old times people have thought that love and hate are complementary opposites, both relative, both transitory. Most religions of the world have said and continue to say, "Beyond such small love, understand Love with a capital L: ultimate, eternal, absolute Love." And they preach, "Love your enemy," "Kill your ego," "Do not commit adultery," and so on. But if we think in this way, we walk in the direction of a nihilism that denies human possibility. At the end of this path there are only two gates to open, one leads to a romantic idea of heaven, the other to a mysterious darkness.

If we correctly solve the problem of jealousy, the arguments of most religions will be cleared up like mist blown away by the wind. Feeling jealous is not bad; rather, it is a good thing. When what we ought to feel is jealous, if we can feel jealous, it is proof that we are healthy, sincere about our own life, and undoubtedly understanding love to be one of the most important matters.

There are people who cannot understand what it is to feel jealous. That is reasonable if they are as pure as babies and living happy married lives, loving their partners and being loved by their partners so that they don't know jealousy. But the surprising thing is that there are people who don't know jealousy who are neither babies nor happy. They couldn't marry their first lover, or couldn't continue their first marriage, yet they say, "What is jealousy? I never felt such a thing." "I mean, don't you have suffering if your husband betrays you?" I ask them. "Betrays me? What do you mean by betray?" "For instance, if your wife kisses another man's lips, don't you feel anything is wrong?" "Wrong? Why? After all she has her own life." "So, you don't mind even if she sleeps with another man?" "Well, that is her freedom." And these people sleep with other people without feeling anything is wrong. They feel only pleasure, they say. I think such people don't know what love is, and so they naturally don't know what jealousy is.

Without love no one can feel jealous. If there is love, when love is endangered, people can feel jealous. If we love a person, we want to be loved by that person. The more we love a person, the more we wish to be loved by that person. The more seriously we love a person, the more sensitive our sense of jealousy becomes. To explain why, I think I should say what love is.

Love is the name for the process of uniting oneself with another self. In order to unite two individual selves, we have to take off our shell of ego, which is enveloping our purity. Purity has no form and isn't bound by the laws of the world of phenomena. Only this purity can unite itself with another purity. Therefore, love starts to have its life when we have the wish to unite ourselves with another, and love will reach its ultimate stage when we fulfill that wish. During the development of love, we have to purify ourselves by denying our form, which is our ego, and when we can unite with another purified self, we begin to use our form very effectively. So making love physically should be the natural result of our love, not the beginning by any means.

Married life is the best situation in which to perform this love. To do so, we need one partner continuously. If there are two or three partners, our effort to perform love will be not be concentrated and we will never see love performed.

Performing love is not like catching fireflies. It is a very hard, lifelong work, worthy of all the energy of our life.

Now, most of what we need to do to attain the ultimate stage of love we already know about instinctively. To reach this stage one of our endeavors is to possess our partner. Without succeeding at possessing our partner, we cannot say we did our best for our love. This desire to possess isn't a shameful matter at all. In fact it is necessary for performing the one common work of loving and being loved by each other. By possessing each other, a married couple vow not to betray each other and vow never to give up trying to attain their ultimate love together. Only people who don't realize this great common work of married life can say such nonsense as, "Possessing is a bad desire and greedily egotistical." People should be aware that our ego seeks to attain higher things than it already has.

By possessing each other, a married couple can make their best effort to be joyfully united. Their wedding is for setting out on a long, hard journey to seek nothing less than each other's purity. Each partner should help and encourage the other on this journey until the purity of both can be united into one. The reward of attaining this ultimate stage of love is unspeakably wonderful. The results of love then come out naturally, spontaneously, without any more effort. Each partner's form will become the great expression of their love.

The feeling of jealousy arises in the course of this journey if one partner doesn't make his or her best effort for their common purpose. The more sincere a married couple is, the more often the problem of jealousy will arise. A sincere couple must make very sure when they marry that their marriage is the true start of this journey. To judge whether it is true, we have to see our loyalty to each other. "Once I marry you, by any means I will not betray you and I vow to do my best to attain our common task, which is to unite ourselves." There must be more or less this much determination. If people can start their marriage in this way, they can be quite happy, and this happiness isn't a self-dreamed, empty matter.

However, serious people might notice that even at the start of their marriage they already feel jealous. This jealousy is over their partner's past. Especially if their partner, whether previously married or not, had sex with another person, they should feel jealous. Since it belongs to the past and since that past contains their beloved partner's matters, they cannot hate it, cannot be angry, but must sadly feel jealous. Jealousy over one's partner's past is felt as regret

with the sense of sadness and sympathy.

"Why did you do such a thing with another person? You and that person didn't think about love at all. You may have thought, but it was too shallow. Love can't be attained by a playing mind, it is a hard task," we may say to such a marriage partner who has had sex in the past. It seems as if we are blaming our partner, but it is not blame. It is lamentation. "Too bad you had a past that didn't work out. My wish is to make you much happier with me. I wish I could have known you in your past and that I could have protected you from your mistake and that we could have begun our journey then, much earlier," we think. This kind of blame-like lamentation is a kind of jealousy.

This kind of jealousy over one's partner's past is not a bad thing, even though it pertains to past matters. "Nothing can be done for one's past," most people think. This isn't true at all. Our past has the power to create our present and our future. If our past is correctly dealt with now, it will live in our present very usefully and effectively. We shouldn't give up trying to make our past live well. Dealing with our past shouldn't be done imprudently, because whether our past is useful or not, enjoyable or not, utterly depends on how we deal with it in the present.

"What is wrong with having had sex before I met you? I thought then I was doing my best. I have no regret about my past life. I respect my past experience and naturally I will keep the things given by that person, photographs taken together and all other mementos." "Don't you feel anything is wrong if our child sees your old photographs of you with another person? Can you with pride show your children a picture in which you are having sex with another person?"

People who say that they have no regret but instead respect their own past must be able to show such a photo to their child.

If they must conceal their past they are better off having confession clearly and starting a new life. Otherwise we will think that such a person isn't a suitable partner with whom to marry and perform our important life of love. Without having regret, no one can use his or her past correctly. We must carry our past through all our life. The person who wishes to use his or her past most effectively and meaningfully must have regret and confess it. This is the determination and vow to be loyal in one's new married life.

"By my ignorance I committed unsuitable acts in my past. I wish that my past will not interfere with my new married life to attain our ultimate love." Thinking thus and doing whatever nice thing can be done is the only way to use one's past usefully and to cure the partner's jealousy about the past. If we don't act correctly, our partner's jealousy will turn to hate and he or she will decide, "This isn't my marriage partner."

The person who doesn't regret and confess the past is stimulating his or her partner's jealousy. Jealousy has to come up in order to protect their good married life. Stimulating another person's jealousy and not solving it is a failing. Such a person will never have a deep, happy married life. And people who don't care, who can't feel even jealous about their partner's life, aren't thinking of their married life, which ought to be the greatest part of human life. Vomitfully, too many people who can't feel even jealous are thinking they are living married life. They are unworthy of being called spiritual animals.

If people can understand what I have said about jealousy over the marriage partner's past, they can tell what I would like to say about the jealousy that occurs in married life. There are many silly, hateful, less-than-animal-like couples who betray each other in their married life. Have they no sense of jealousy?

Generally they do, but they are too weak to confront it. They are living without thinking about love and life. They don't notice that they are ignoring their worthy life and that they are polluting the world. Those who have the ability to feel jealous should enjoy it because they have the possibility of finding the life of love. They shouldn't be charmed by the thoughtless acts and sayings of those people who have no sense of jealousy or who can't face their jealousy. By their shameless cowardice they will teach the same nihilism as old religions taught us. Respect the sense of jealousy, which is a highly intelligent as well as instinctive treasure, and build a bright and warm human society.

Anger

Ever since the time I began to form my independent self, I have felt as much anger as there are leaves on a tree. But to recall any such instance without regret is as hard as to find an orange on an apple tree.

Often, late at night in my dark bed, when I am reminded of those people who received my anger — their sorrowful faces, pure like white lilies — it makes my underarms wet with cold sweat.

One of the least recommendable things in our married life is to be angry at our marriage partner. With our anger why should we give one more unhappiness to our beloved partner? As it is, he or she has to live with countless sufferings. Bring out that fat happy Chinese god and shower upon him our thousand tons of anger; he won't mind, he exists for this purpose, and will continue his vast, ageless laugh. But to our marriage partner we should not anger.

We know we can change fire to useful energy. Can't we change our anger to useful and creative love? It is possible only if we observe and understand the life of our partner more than we understand ourselves. Not seeing and not caring about our partner and blinding ourselves with the flame of self-pity and self-complacence is our anger. So, although controlling and restricting ourselves is important, our primary effort should be given to observing the sad nature of our partner. Unless we deeply see the sad features of our partner, we cannot prevent the germination of our anger.

The reason that seeing the sadness of our partner helps us to extinguish our anger is that it brings us to a field where there is no unfairness, where the condition, situation, and existence of us each is the same. As soon as we see the deep sadness within our partner, we will see him or her in the same light by which we see ourselves. Then, we can have no reason to be angry with our partner; there are no demands, no over-expectations, no assumptions, no accusations, and no contempt. Instead, the wish will arise in us to protect, educate, and encourage our partner. These are parts of the content of our love.

Coming back from hard work to find his wife lying on a couch in front of the television, peanut shells scattered around and nothing for supper may make a husband angry. But why shouldn't he see her situation, reasons, cause for doing so? Even if he can make no sense out of her superficial daily life, at least he must be able to see the sadness within her if he notices the fact that she is almost hypnotized by beginningless ignorance.

A husband may consume hours just to make a shelf in the kitchen and finally, at the sound of many dishes and cups crashing, his wife dashes to the kitchen and gazes at him furiously. But why doesn't she see the sadness in him by realizing that her husband is incapable of this sort of task, as bad as she is or worse?

A husband spends every evening busily scheming for his holiday, "working, working," and on the morning of the holiday, his friends barely drop in to greet his wife and children before taking him away. As soon as he slides into the car, they set off, leaving behind only gas exhaust and his dirty shoes and shirts. No wife can welcome such a husband when he returns in the evening, inviting his friends in for a drink and a smoke. However, this is the very time when a wife should observe the sad nature of her husband. At least, it isn't the time for her to be angry but rather the time she should sincerely discover the sadness in her husband if she wishes their married life will become the greenhouse of their love, trust, and respect.

People may think that of course cases so comical and cheap as these are almost unworthy of anger. But regardless of whether

a person is watching TV, or performing on a violin, or doing whatever it is that gives personal satisfaction, if on account of it his or her partner angers, it is all the same; any situation can ignite anger, but we should have no reason to justify our anger. Anger proves what tiny love we have.

However, I am not at all saying that people should be excused when they create situations that anger their partner. I am saying that the partner who feels anger should take the honorable, initiating role of building up their love, their married life. Facing the situation in which one has reason to be angry with one's partner is a great opportunity, because it is a time to see the partner's deep nature, sadness, which becomes visible like a green mountain in the clearing mist. We can see if we just concentrate on observing him or her.

Cheated, lied to, used without respect? Kicked, beaten, betrayed! Well, whichever of us does such a nearly fatal act in married life, it isn't always too late to compress our anger and fix it to a rocket and shoot it into the void. It may enjoy the same fate as a falling star.

Therefore, even if our partner betrays us and even uses our own master bed — while our children are in the next room — to sleep with another person, shouldn't we fairly observe why our partner betrayed us? We must regret that we couldn't satisfy our partner. We must see the sad want of our partner and rather go to help find his or her happiness instead of being angry. The only secret by which we can convert our rootless pride to human confidence is the concentration of our energy into the act of understanding another person's life.

The person who has already become angry or who cannot free himself or herself from anger, having a very small fuse, is also a very sad person. Reflect with cold sweat — it will encourage a love for one's partner ten times greater than the anger felt. I hope the time will come when anger is heard no more even if cold sweat floods the world.

Sexual Desire in Marriage

In our married life, sexual desire has its suitable place, which we should recognize through our own experience. I see no reason why we should ignore or deny our sexual desire, and I have no reason to admire people who stimulate or encourage it. Both ways, evading our sexual desire and extolling it, are the same in that they don't respect the harmonious life that will be attained when our various desires all have their suitable place. Each individual desire should be given freedom to function so far as it doesn't invade and disrupt the total harmony of all our desires.

Sexual desire itself is neither a shadowy sinful thing nor bright and admirable. It is rather neutral and yet a profound and mysterious being like the quiet water of a mountain lake. However, if we don't control it to attain a better purpose for our life, it can become a lone creature that vigorously runs only to satisfy its meaningless energy, and that can't be corralled by our reason and is harmful to our own life as well as to others. We cannot trust anything that doesn't enjoy coexisting with our reason. Our sexual desire uncontrolled is like the fire set by a person whose only pleasure is to see destruction too big to be extinguished by the tears that come into our eyes when we have an extreme longing to see a trustable, everlasting world filled with love. Our sexual desire should be controlled, because not controlling it leads to cultivating a destructive weapon to destroy our life.

Normally in marriage our sexual relation with our partner is assuming its important and basic role. We can't think of being married without any sexual relation. And if this sexual relation breaks, our marriage relation also faces danger, especially if one partner begins to engage in sex outside of marriage. As we become older, our sexual desire weakens and, conversely, our interest in other matters grows stronger. But as long as our sexual relation is so important to our married life, we would do best to study what sexual desire is, what kind of place it should be given, and how we should control it. Otherwise we may have trouble in our married life caused by our own sexual desire. If we don't consider it until we become old, we can't help ourselves solve the problems it raises; delay doesn't solve anything, and the incurable fact remains with its pull, like the gravity of the earth.

Our sexual desire in its primitive stage doesn't discriminate in its choice of object; its object can be almost anyone of the opposite sex. Because of this rather thoughtless generosity of our sexual desire, we can marry relatively easily, at least as far as our sexual desire is concerned. But for the same reason the stability of our married life can often be threatened. Therefore, if we wish to live a successful married life, we have to be able to limit the capability of this generous, aimless sexual desire and concentrate it upon one object, which is our marriage partner. Concentration is possible when we refuse to see ourselves subjectively. Instead we must try to see our partner subjectively and not objectively. That is to say, in married life our sexual desire must be satisfied with our marriage partner only because and when our partner wants to satisfy his or her sexual desire.

Such a sexual relation in our married life, passive for

ourselves but very active for our partner, can amend another
primitive peculiarity of our sexual desire, which is its exceedingly

egoistic character. Our sexual desire at its primitive level has
great concern for itself and almost no concern for its object.
When people remind themselves of their youth, particularly their
adolescence, they can see this desire so expressed. At that age,
what kind of selfish dream did they create to satisfy their sexual
desire? Didn't they imagine as they liked the time, place, and acts
of their sexual objects without any permission from them?

Our sexual desire has little concern for its object but
earnestly seeks its own satisfaction. Unless it is controlled by our
reason, it doesn't care about a suitable method for attaining its
satisfaction, doesn't think what effect will come after it has been
satisfied. This behavior of our sexual desire should be carefully
guided in our married life. In married life, our sexual desire

should be a pleasurable, useful, and bright matter and it should contribute to making a better married life. Therefore our sexual desire must satisfy itself in responding to our partner rather than in demanding from our partner.

If we seek to satisfy our own sexual desire when there is no corresponding need in our marriage partner, sooner or later we have to realize that our married life is not doing well. This is because we demand unwelcome work from our partner. By the uncomfortable sacrifice of our partner, even if we satisfy our own sexual desire, how can we enjoy our married life? Such a one-way sexual relationship can send a chilly draft through our married life.

Having Sex without Hoping
for Childbirth

Normally we enjoy sexual relations in our married life. We have sexual desire instinctively to create a new life that will inherit our life. The difference between us and animals in this respect is that animals have sex only to satisfy their instinctive desire to preserve their own species, whereas for the most part we human beings don't have sex solely to preserve our species. In fact, in these ages we scarcely have sex for its original purpose, but rather just to satisfy our sexual nerves. Often we deny the ability of our generative organs and use our sexual organs independent of them. It is like enjoying the flowers of trees but not welcoming the fruit. So, generally we make an effort to stimulate our sexual organs as well as some effort to paralyze our generative organs. When we see ourselves as animals among other animals in nature, certainly these efforts are self-contradictory.

Whether it is good or bad, putting ourselves in contra-dictions is our peculiarity. All our sufferings come from these contradictions. We don't suffer if we have sex to have our child, because in that there is no contradiction. But we must create some problems if we have sex without any wish to have a child. Various questions arise: Is it nice, beautiful, and worthy to have sex without wanting but rather refusing a child? Have we the right to refuse the life that would come naturally without using birth control? Is it correct to cause an abortion? And so on.

All these problems will be solved in our married life if we make sure of the correct understanding about three things: 1) having children, 2) the meaning of sexual relations, and 3) birth control and abortion.

First, about having children. In married life, one of our highest enjoyments is to have children. We were all children once, and without having children of our own we can't become parents. Only being a child and not knowing parenthood is an imperfect life. It is like forever seeing a green tomato and never knowing a ripened one. It is a very sorrowful situation that there are people who can't have a child for some reason even though they want to, because married life without a child is like a house without any light. There is no better treasure than our child. No silver or gold can replace the value of a child. For the individual person, from a subjective viewpoint, having one's own child is the greatest possible creation. Married life without a child compared to married life with a child is like a two-dimensional world compared to a three-dimensional world.

To live a worthy, profound married life, the best thing for us is to welcome our baby who gives us other dimensions of life. Without a child we can't study our own past spent in childhood, and can't study our own parents who took care of us. By having a child we will experience the enjoyment of doing for another and the suffering given by another. With our child our humanity has the chance to grow fully.

Having children is one vivid effect of our married life. Married life with no effect is like a fruit tree with no fruit. The poor effect proves that the cause, the marriage, is poor.

If married life is going well, don't both partners want a child created by themselves together? The more we love our marriage partner, the more we want to know all of our partner's past life. We want to live together in the same time and place. Our love increases by knowing each other's past, our trust increases by wishing to share the same life in the future, and our respect increases by doing our best in the present. Having each other's child is the harmonious conduct of this love, trust, and respect. So, if a married couple thinks sincerely about their married life, they naturally will say to each other, "I want to have your child." For such people, having sex is a bright, pleasurable, and meaningful act.

The second thing we have to think about is the meaning of sexual relations, because there are married couples who don't want to have children. Some have had a child already and others haven't yet. In either case they don't want to have a child now, even though they like having sexual relations with each other. Having sexual relations without hoping to have a child is a self-contradictory act. "I like to have sex with you but I don't want to have your child," each marriage partner must say in such a contradictory situation. This is certainly a funny marriage relationship. Marrying only to have sexual relations instead of hoping to have children is not different from masturbating or having a hired prostitute.

By any means, living only to satisfy our sexual desire isn't an admirable matter. It is like eating food only for the pleasure of tasting. Eating food should be done for maintaining the energy necessary to achieve some worthy cultural creation. The same thing can be said of having sex. If we marry we can have children as the result of sex. Not hoping to see the effect while enjoying the cause is a queer thing, like the dream of a schizophrenic.

There must be something wrong with such a marriage. People shouldn't become slaves of their sexual organs. People shouldn't marry only to satisfy their sexual desire. By satisfying our sexual desire we don't attain any worthy thing but must sacrifice a lot of useful ability and time. To satisfy only sexual desire we cause troubles and pollute the world, as we can see by the daily proof in front of us. Therefore it is better for people not to indulge in their sexual relations without hoping for children. Spend such energy and time for more worthy matters. If there are people who think this world isn't a suitable world for our children to live in because it is much too rotten, poor, and dangerous a place, they would be better off spending their energy and ability preparing a better world for the next generation instead of only satisfying their sexual desire and not hoping for a child of their own.

However, most people while they are mentally as well as physically young like to satisfy their sexual desire without hoping for children. This isn't an admirable matter. But if they can't control their desire, having sex enjoyably with their marriage partner isn't an especially bad thing. As long as they can satisfy their sexual desire and while it isn't harmful to other human activities and people, they can have sex with the awareness that "we are having sex only to satisfy our desire and not for other reasons." If people have sexual relations with their marriage partner without spending so much time and energy, it makes a cheerful, bright, and peaceful enough life. People must take care, however, not to do too much or too little. In this world the middle way should be the way.

For those people who don't want to have children and want to have only sexual relations, there is one thing they should give up, which is the wish to perfect sexual orgasm. It can be perfected only in a married life that is working well, in which both partners want to have children and can have sexual relations enjoyably. Do not expect to attain perfect orgasm without hoping for a child. In such a contradictory act we can temporarily calm down our sexual desire, and we must feel some sadness at seeing our inability to control our desire.

There are meanings in having sexual relations without hoping for children. The biggest meaning is not that of satisfying our sexual desire. It is that by having sexual relations we can see ourselves. Have sex with open eyes and see who we are. This study will be fruitful for us and we will find our human way to live, not like holy spirits and not like devils.

The third thing we have to think about is birth control and abortion. The reason we need various means of birth control is that we don't appreciate new life that might otherwise come while we are wanting only sexual relations.

Cutting off the possibility of new life isn't an enjoyable thing to do. It is like putting seeds on a rock. At the same time there are quite a few people who strongly hope to have children and yet cannot. Using birth control is a meaningless luxury for them. Before discussing whether it is good or bad to destroy the possibility of new lives, shouldn't we feel sad for the lives prevented from coming by our artificial will? If people have some imagination, can't they see numerous floating spirits in the dark, which have the possibility of being born into this world but are having their ropes for climbing up to this world cut off? If people can have a little intelligence, enough to recognize a certain insect in the grasses just by hearing the sound in the autumn night, they probably can imagine numerous spirits not welcomed to this world. When we use birth control to satisfy our sexual desire, we shouldn't put aside our intellectual imagination. I hope people will understand that the basic tone running beneath our sexual desire is a faintly sorrowful, pure sadness. Sexual desire isn't always a bright and pleasurable desire to be chased after by us.

Causing abortion is definitely a sin regardless of whether or not it is a crime, because we are killing independent life, by our will, for our sake. Even if we kill our unborn child to save our own life we should regret it. We have to see our ego in choosing our life instead of the life of another. Even a person who loses a child unwillingly by some unknown cause or by a reasonable known cause must regret and feel sorrow for the unborn child who died, because the life of the unborn child is as respectable as our own, if not more so. We must regret and feel sorrow, and do our best for the unborn child. Otherwise we are slighting life and we will live without realizing the value of even our own life. Our married life shouldn't become a slaughterhouse for numerous possibilities of unknown lives and unborn children who began to live in this world.

Even if we cause abortion unwillingly, we should regret our incapability, our ignorance, and our ego. If we can feel sorrow for the unborn child we wanted who died, how much more we should cry, should deserve punishment, if we cause abortion willingly.

Otherwise we won't be forgiven by the killed unborn child even if we build ten hundred churches on the sandy soil, even if we invent the elixir of life by studying millions of phenomena. No unborn child killed by us will be satisfied unless we build a formless church in our mind. What is this formless church in our mind? If we want to know, we must first live a correct married life, which will train us to know what the mind is. Without such training, our asking for the church or temple is ridiculous and no one has any medicine to cure us. Suppose a person stands on a riverside and says, "Hey, look! What a dirty, polluted river! Plastic cups and bottles on the oily water!" If he then throws his cigarette butt into the current, push him in. There is no better help you can give him.

Religious Differences between Husband and Wife

Marriage partners who don't understand what real religion is may raise some problems between themselves when they have different religions. No one on this earth needs to believe any religion if it causes a quarrel. If we have to see blood, whether spiritual or physical, for the sake of religion, we would be better off jumping back to a primitive age over the heads of Adam and Eve.

The person who discusses another person's goodness or badness is the person suited to be criticized for his goodness or badness. Any kind of true religion teaches us to seek that which isn't invaded by worldly and relative standards of value. Religions show us that truth exists for us when we go beyond our dualistic world of phenomena such as individual age, position, situation, sex, nationality, and all sorts of conflicting contrasts.

Nevertheless, the reason we occasionally have to see some quarrels caused by religious differences is understandable. It is mainly because most religious leaders in the past and present have failed utterly to teach us what real religion is while they splendidly succeeded in teaching what religious phenomena are. Try to ask anyone about the doctrines, moralities, history, functions, customs, costumes, festivals, or utensils of any kind of religion and you will have as easy a time getting an answer as you would if you asked a New Yorker where the Empire State Building is. Even a five-year-old can tell with bright eyes what Christmas is as a religious phenomenon, but who at eighty years can sufficiently say what the true meaning of Christmas is as the essence of the Christian religion?

Studying religious phenomena can be a way to understand religion, certainly; but we should be ready to throw away the things we study as soon as they begin to obstruct the way to reach real religion or as soon as they force us to contradict our religion. It is a disappointingly difficult matter to tell what real religion is. However, I believe that no religion teaches us to fight, and that every religion agrees we should love one another. Isn't this enough information about what religion is? Anyone who can understand this much has the ability to reach the world of real religion through his or her sincere life.

Marriage partners who must quarrel because they have different religions should create a new religion for themselves instead of preserving or insisting on their old religions, which were mostly taught to them in their childhood by their parents and society. If they have the energy to fight, they must have the energy to create. After all, marriage partners face a new situation, which they never experienced before they married, so they have new needs for their religion, too. If their old, inherited religions have no authority, they must begin to complain about the imperfections and the faults of each other's old religions. In such a case, if they have no fresh desire and courage to create a new, mutually useful religion for themselves, they will be tortured by the ghosts of their old religions. And their married life will be carried away by insentient floating waves farther and farther from the shore of a real religion.

They have to realize especially in their situation that the life of religion is active only when it is in the process of being newly created. If, however, a religion needs to be maintained by great effort, needs to be insisted upon, and needs to be preserved even if it causes quarrels, then it is in a dying condition. Why shouldn't we enjoy our married life with the enjoyment of creating a new religion that has living power for us, that will be exclusively for our own married life, that will be a fountain to cure the thirst of society?

When a married couple newly creates their religion, the most important thing is that they both practice it, no matter what their ideas are about it. And if they cannot practice it, they must adjust it for themselves. However, if they adjust it too much to their low ability, it will no longer be religion. In such a case, no quarrel need arise over their old religions because they have no ability to think about religion. So they have no reason to dream about having a new religion for themselves. At this time I am writing for the people who have quarrels arising from religious differences, because they have the ability to fight, and for the people who want to create a new religion for the sake of their peace, happiness, and sincere, worthy life throughout their married life.

Don't Tell Anyone

Neither in principle nor in practice should we think it right to tell others about a person's private matters if he or she doesn't wish them to be known. This is because everyone, except for babies who have no ability to live in this world by themselves, has some secrets, and these secrets are so important to the person concerned that they are often elements that compose his or her very life. One's secret is like a chestnut in its bur, that is, it isn't a thing to be opened by force from the outside, but will rather open of its own accord from within.

To have a worthy married life it is essential that we be irreplaceable as a marriage partner. To become the marriage partner who can't be replaced, we must be trusted by our partner. To gain trust, we must fear to reveal our partner's secrets. We should never be charmed by the cruel impulse to peel off the healing skin of any wound that our marriage partner has. We shouldn't be so dull as to speak up carelessly about matters that our partner doesn't enjoy but only gets pain from having revealed.

Therefore people who want to have a profound, happy married life must vow at their wedding, or now if they are already married and haven't yet vowed, that they will never reveal any matters that either of them doesn't wish to have revealed. Each can emphasize with confidence, "I will never tell anyone anything you won't enjoy. Even if you have committed a crime such as stealing or murder, you can be assured that your crime will not be exposed by me."

Some people, especially those who are concerned about society, may raise the question, "Isn't it going too far not to report a crime committed by one's marriage partner? There's a law against giving sanctuary to criminals."

It is a very difficult question. It becomes a dilemma as to whether we should choose to trust our marriage partner or society. Nevertheless, once we marry, we should choose our marriage partner. What does it mean to marry? To marry means to live together, to share our life. Isn't it the holiest of holy processes to unify two different lives into one life? Married life is not for flattering present society and not for maintaining the conventional world. It is for amending present society and creating a better world. Marriage, a true married life, is necessary for concentrating our good wish to make a better world. It is possible to make a better world if people live a healthy married life, studying each other to know who they are, not God and not beasts, and to know what love is, not separated from trust and respect.

Have we ever had a society that could be called trustworthy? Before and after Christ, the claims of so-called society have always continued to warrant suspicion. But who can doubt the beauty of the person who bets his or her life to keep his or her partner's trust? How can a person who cannot gain complete trust even from his or her marriage partner gain real trust from society? People who have married, shared all from bed to frying pan, done everything together from sex to prayer, should enjoy the punishment received from society for not revealing their marriage partner's secret, even if doing so is a social crime. This kind of contradiction will happen because our society isn't a society made by people who can devote their lives to the beauty of trust. A large part of our society is made up of people who easily betray even their own marriage partners, people who are too self-loving to live for others.

Until society is brought to life by people who understand that trust is one of the most important matters for us, we should practice the life of trust in our individual married lives, and should be careful not to marry with an untrustworthy person. And we should encourage the person who wants to gain trust. If a criminal is arrested by the police because of notification given by the criminal's marriage partner, should we be glad or should we cry? In either case, we shouldn't cover our eyes from seeing the beauty of the person who goes to jail for not reporting to the police the crime of his or her marriage partner.

In daily married life it is very important not to tell on our marriage partner. If we tell, we prove we are not loving, not respecting, and not trusting our partner. Moreover, we prove we are marrying only to use our marriage partner to our advantage. If we live such a cheating and shallow married life, the people surrounding us will come between us and will lead our married life into a chaotic and ugly place of war. Why? Because surrounding people instinctively know that to get some profit they should tear down friendship and cause fighting. Whatever profit the people around us want to get, we are better off protecting our married life.

Which of our marriage partner's matters we shouldn't tell others isn't something I know, but it should be known by each marriage partner. However, here are some examples and my feelings about them, which may be useful sometime for someone.

1)   Some people tell their parents about their marriage quarrels. I think such people are foolish. Parents have a kind of

magnet to pull back their child, and it grows stronger when a married couple quarrels. This magnet is never useful to unite a married couple, but on the contrary is effective to divorce them from each other.

2)   Some people speak to their friends of how incapable or stupid their marriage partner is. My comment is that such people are at least as incapable or stupid, if not more so.

3)   Some talk proudly about their marriage partner. "How about you?" I would like to ask such a person.

4)   Some talk of how their marriage partner is making a great effort or receiving suffering. "If you have time to talk about such a thing, go to help your marriage partner. Effort and suffering are shade-loving plants and should not be exposed."

5)   Sometimes people confess to, or consult with, a teacher or priest about married life. "Come to me together," I'll say, at least if I am a priest or teacher for them.

Concealing Nothing

One's privacy should be respected in the same way as an unborn baby is provided a secure womb. To form and organize ourselves into independent, responsible, and meaningful creatures we must have the time and place to concentrate our own vitality. Without concentration we can't have a life of knowing either ourselves or the people and things surrounding us.

However, in our married life, respecting privacy shouldn't be confused with concealing the truth from each other. Privacy in its best usage is necessary to prepare ourselves for serving others, so the final goal of respecting privacy is to contribute to the happiness of others. But concealing the truth is the effect and future cause of distrust between partners, so naturally it detracts from the happiness of them both. If marriage partners trust each other, there will be no reason to conceal anything from each other. The less the truth is concealed, the more trust is built up, and the better the married life that follows. After all, trust is one of the most important elements for our steady, lasting, and pleasurable married life.

Nevertheless, why do we conceal things or hide or even lie to our marriage partner? Why do we sometimes judge that not exposing the truth is better, even though it later proves to be a poor judgment since nothing is stronger than the honest truth and the building up of trust? In married life in particular, there are two reasons we feel we must conceal the truth, no matter what. The first is that there is no strong, common wish in both partners to construct married life on the foundation of trust, or no realization that anything built on sand is an illusory palace. Second, we are loving an illusion instead of the person who really is our partner.

As long as these two dark groves aren't cultivated and clearly bathed in sunlight, we will always have to conceal something

from each other in our married relation. The fault quite fairly rests with both partners and both should be fairly blamed. The misery of concealing the truth is not only that of the person from whom it is concealed but also that of the person who has to conceal it.

Building our married life on trust must be done by both beloved partners, little by little. It is a very difficult task, because everything on this earth is, in a word, sand. Nothing lasts eternally, all is changeable, breakable, dependent on other such forms or situations. Marriage partners have to find in each other and in their relation the thing that lasts forever, does not change, does not break, and is not swayed by others, which is trust. Is there such a thing? Even if there is, can we find it?

These worries aren't questions that can be answered by any person outside of the marriage partners. They should try to answer between themselves. My wife and I have questions for ourselves and we have answers for ourselves, not for other couples. If you want answers given by an outsider, get them from him or her, live for him or her, and give up living for yourselves. I am not a vampire who sucks the blood of others by giving my answer to them. Think what trust is while you are in the arms of your partner, while you walk, go to the toilet, after hitting a long shot at golf, sometimes together with your partner in a comfortable, quiet living room or on a hillside from where you can look down over the sea through a pine forest.

It is sad if we are loving an illusion, not because we realize that we are deceived by our partner but because our partner is never truly loved. There is a legend in which a fox appears as a beautiful woman and a man falls in love with it. When this man awakes from his daydream, he regrets how stupid he was to love such a beast and so waste his valuable time. He is very foolish, but if he doesn't cry for this actual fox that was never loved at all by him and if he cries only over his own silliness, we have to see his cruelty as well as his foolishness. Needless to say, we shouldn't think that loving our partner's dress, name, or social position is love. And loving some particular gesture, manner, or habit of our partner is not real love. Without knowing really what is going on in the brain and body of our partner, without any care about our partner's past and future, hidden from the formal surface, we will end up loving an illusion.

Therefore if we wish to live a married life free of concealment, we must concentrate on each other's life more than on any other thing. Our ideal is to see our marriage partner's life from the bottom of hell to the top of heaven.

Realizing Commonness

Partners in marriage who fail to realize the profound commonness that is latent yet capable of vigorously acting in each other's lives have to face a shallow, meaningless, unexciting, and unsatisfied married life. We are able to marry with almost anyone when we see the surface similarities of our bodies, actions, and situations, while our differences are hidden or unperceived. However, such superficial similarities cannot sustain our married life, and of course aren't able to bring our married life into the core of our universe, which is the base and the reason to live our life. This is because these lucky and accidental similarities soon fade, lose their value for each partner, and rather begin to rival one another. In consequence, the underlying differences of each partner come up sharply, which is to say, these differences cease to be charming or possible to dismiss as they were at the start of marriage, because there is no realized profound commonness making an appreciation of the differences possible.

The similarities between partners aren't unwelcome. Rather, they can be welcome, but people should be aware that similarities have no creative power to contribute to their married life. This is because similarities are attained individually, regardless of the other marriage partner, and one's so-called past fate takes credit for them. The similarities each partner sees in the other, such as nationality, language, cultural background, family air, economic condition, physical peculiarity, education and work career, hobby, taste, manner and gesture, are matters that haven't been attained by married life together; rather, they were attained before the couple began association for marriage, without any love and work between them. Naturally these similarities have no trace of each partner's love in them. Therefore we have no profound and subjective interest in them, and no concern, or we are unable to have, even if we wish. We are able to admire the partner who has similarities, but we can't be that partner; we are able to sympathize with the partner who has similarities, but in this way we can't reduce the distance between ourselves to zero and be united. So each partner must all the time be aware of the absolute distance or difference between the object, his or her partner, and the subject, himself or herself. Unless we have love that we have made together, unless we have shared our blood in suffering, agony, and effort, we can't be each other no matter how similar our similarities are. The similarities of our partner can be objects of our interest, care, sympathy, admiration — love, if we call it so — as well as objects of our disinterest, unconcern, intolerance, contempt — hatred, if we call it so. To the extent that we see these similarities favorably, we are able to be charmed, and are able to love each other and able to marry. But this love for similarities gives continuous stimulation to our disappointment at the realization that we are perceiving only the surface of love. So if we wish to live a successful married life we would do better not to give such great value to these similarities, or at least we have to be aware that they have no creative power for our married life. Yet most of us cannot even marry unless we see similarities, some or many, and seeing too many differences doesn't at all help us to marry. Certainly, seeing similarities helps us to marry. Let us start our fire with a match.

Once we marry and as soon as we marry, for the happiness of our married life it is valuable to determine not to depend on our similarities. Rather we must determine to realize our profound commonness with each other, which will be made, protected, and nursed exclusively by us, for our sake, in our situation. What sort of thing can be our commonness is to be discovered by each couple, not, needless to say, by each person

independently. This profound commonness is the power to create a happy married life, is the reason why we live married life. This profound commonness leads, encourages, gives moral self-direction, gives power to persevere, and satisfies the married couple. Without such profound commonness, our married life will be meaningless, wasteful, painful, irritable, unsatisfied, full of all sorts of wholesale human misery.

Each couple should understand and believe that profound commonness is their Bible, their Constitution, and no other thing is greater in its importance for them. Marriage partners who haven't yet realized profound commonness will be better off if they give greater effort to finding it, or they must fear the destruction of their married life. At least such partners can think sincerely that their profound commonness is to realize the unknown profound commonness. Most happily married people are able to think that raising their children, succeeding at work in the social world, creating some kinds of art, discovering some useful truth, etc., is their profound commonness. There is no reason that any kind of couple cannot realize their profound commonness if they love each other and want to live a worthy life and wish to contribute some happiness for mankind. It will always help if each partner asks what way of life is the best way to bring alive the life of the other partner on this earth.

Thanks and Complaints

Generally, having thanks is one element of our satisfactory life and it contributes to maintaining the stability of our life, regardless of whether our life should be amended or not. This is so because 1) we feel thanks when we imagine situations in which we might be unable to enjoy some present advantage, 2) when we thus feel thanks we are kicking away our impulsive complaints about things we lack, and therefore 3) our thanks satisfies us, and the power emanating from it maintains our condition, whereas our complaints dissatisfy us and the power emanating from them creates a new condition.

So, we can neither recommend that people live only in the light radiated by thanks, poetically describing meadow and forest, bird and animal, nor recommend that they live only wrinkled by complaints, running around barefoot in a turkey thicket. We must always live in the balance of contradictions. Finding the balance where we can stand serene is our work, which should be our pleasure when it can be performed with our marriage partner.

Now, in our married life we must be able to thank our partner freely as well as complain freely. The person who recommends that another person feel thanks must be equally ready to recommend that another person complain. There are so-called religious, self-authorized people past and present who teach us to feel only thanks for everything given by an irresistible power, and not to complain about anything, not even about things created by man's evil will. They must be criticized for wishing too much that people live under their authority and be governed as an uncreative, static society.

Certainly feeling thanks brings us satisfaction, but satisfaction isn't the only thing we must seek. What we particularly should not seek is a satisfaction combined with calm. Instead what we hope to gain is complaint with calmness, and satisfaction with creative movement. How can we have such a vital balance of thanks and complaints in our married life?

First, in our married life we have to realize that thanks and complaints, though they have contradictory effects, arise from the same place in our mind, which dislikes or hates unwelcome conditions. We feel thankful because we fear unwelcome situations that have come or might come to us, even though we are presently in a welcome situation. We feel like complaining when we are presently in an unwelcome situation, especially when we recall the welcome situations we have had or suppose we might have ahead. Whether we express ourselves in thanks or complaints, it is the same happiness we are seeking, with the same wish to escape from misery, to protect, to satisfy, and to nurse our life. Therefore we need not jump to the ceiling for joy at our marriage partner's thanks to us, nor need we mourn and gloomily shelter ourselves in the basement if we receive complaints from our partner. Instead, we quietly and clearly have to understand what our partner is thanking and complaining about and how our partner is expressing these feelings.

Second, both marriage partners must understand what are really worthy and reasonable things to be thankful for or to complain about to each other. In the early stages of married life, a common understanding about this subject is important and the partners who attain this common understanding will prosper in their married life. They can complain to each other just as they can thank each other.

People who wish for the progressive growth of their married life must have courageous and painstaking interest in thanks and complaints. This means that our interest should be in doing things for which we can be thanked rather than in putting ourselves in the position of being thankful, and in being complained about rather than in complaining. The life of thanks is passive and easy when we lose the passion to create a better situation. To live, to work, and to do in a manner worthy of thanks is harder, and so pursuing such a life is the only matter worthy of thanks. Unless it comes as the result of our own will and effort, even if we have something for which we can be thanked, receiving such thanks is vain and inhuman. We openly should live our life to be thanked, and we should do so consciously, with everlasting effort. For such a person who understands the importance of being thanked, it must be plain common sense that being complained about is the whip of love and that there is no reason to escape from it.

Expressions of Love

Married people constantly have to find ways of expressing their love for each other, because unexpressed love is of less use than a dead fox. The idea of love as created in our brain can give some pleasure to us individually, but to no one else. It rather harms our beloved. Who enjoys being shown the blueprint of a house without any means of building it?

Love should be proved, which means expressed. Love that can't be proved, can't be expressed, is as much in vain as the enlightenment of one who is possessed by a blind belief in enlightenment, colder than a frozen iron ladder set against the back of an old brick building. Love that can't be expressed isn't love. It should be called by another name. It can probably be called selfish love, which people should clearly distinguish from love for another person. These two loves often can't be separated, like the color of ocean and sky at the horizon; but although it is so at the horizon, it shouldn't be so at the shoals nearest the shore.

Our love seeks to express itself, and when it gets tired of doing so, that is the time when it is in critically ill condition. Therefore we shouldn't greedily withhold our best effort to express our love. Nothing in this world is eternal; our love also is a mortal thing. Only our strong wish and effort can support the life of our love, can bring it nearer to eternity.

Nothing is unchangeable in this world; love also changes.

Without our effort and wisdom, our love has no direction to go in, but floats on the wave of time and will be drunk by the mouth of a dark and ignorant sea. Our love shouldn't be a weak piece of straw cast onto the river to depend for its movement on the mechanical ripples. Our love shouldn't be a mysterious falling star appearing from the dark and disappearing into the dark. Our love, we hope, should be well perceived, correctly directed, and respectably raised by our effort and wisdom. If we devote ourselves to expressing it, we will see the correct way and the bright, strong life of our love.

Our love for each other can be expressed by using forms, material things. We have to use our physical potential to its fullest, our eyes, nose, ears, mouth, hands, legs, all, for this purpose. We even speak well, choose the most suitable words to express our love. Nonetheless, we will realize that no matter how effectively we use our body, our love isn't expressed fully enough unless we borrow forms other than just our own body. When our marriage partner complains of stiff shoulders we can massage them with our hands, but if our partner cries in thirst, should we stick our finger into his or her throat? Direct use of our body to express our love is certainly of basic importance, but it has its limits. The greater the love we have, the more limits we will realize we have. Our love for our marriage partner shouldn't be so small that it can be well enough expressed by using only our own body.

Actually, our love begins to grow when we definitely recognize the limitations of our own body and willingly begin to borrow other materials such as varieties of food and medicine, clothing and accessories, dwellings and utensils, etc. What we should notice is that the proof of love can be seen in this process by which we try to secure these things for our beloved marriage partner. Naturally if we don't attempt to secure them, or if we don't need to because we already have them, we can't show our love and our love also doesn't grow.

Thus it is that we have to realize our love is quite a physical matter rather than spiritual. In fact, the acts of love may lead us into an unending struggle to seek material things because we can't obtain them as easily as we hope. In addition to simple forms, we want to give various nice situations to our marriage partner, a nice beach house in summer, a mountain cottage in winter, with suitable garden and furniture in each. We want to provide comfortable friends; not only friends, perhaps a certain amount of admirers, assistants. Occasionally news journalists and TV interviewers also must visit us. Otherwise our marriage partner won't see the proof of our love.

In short, a nice situation at each time must be given as proof of our love for our marriage partner. But how many people in this world can achieve this? And if we love, how can we bear to give unpleasant, unhappy, miserable, unwelcome situations? If our marriage partner has a bad situation, how can we be heartless and do nothing about it?

The reason many of our love affairs end in tragedy is not so much our lack of spiritual love or wish to love, but the character of love itself, which seeks forms, material things. Now, the only way to rescue ourselves from the hell of seeking material things with so little possibility of obtaining them depends on the eye of our marriage partner, the eye to read our mind through the material things we borrow to express our love. If our marriage partner has such ability and further cultivates it to see our mind, to see the reason we should express love and seek material things, our love will be saved instead of being killed on the road to seeking forms endlessly.

After all, we only borrow forms to assist our love, for our love should be the master of forms. Our marriage partner must train to see the master of forms, even if the forms provided by us are humble and poor. Some spiritual people can see Buddha or God even in a stem of wild grass. If our marriage partner cannot

see our love in our efforts to obtain nice things, good situations for him or her, our marriage partner is sadly blind. And unfortunately such couples who are blind will kill their love.

Unexpressed love is not love, and blindness to love even when it is imperfectly expressed is also not love. To increase our married love we should try to express our love as concretely as we can, and at once we should try to see our love as spiritually as we can in the forms.

One winter day I was staying at the house of my father-in-law. In the late evening we lost sight of him and all of the family wondered where he had gone. We began to worry about him. Finally he came back, red nosed, his coat collar standing, white breath. We all gathered about him with questions. "I noticed that our son-in-law had run out of his Player cigarettes. I wanted to get them for him but there were none of this brand in the shops in our town. Fortunately I could find them in the next town," he said, and he took out a package of cigarettes from his coat. "You went to the next town for that?" Everyone was astonished.

To Think about Death

Deep love arises from fear of death. The more we fear death, the more we love life. Thinking about the death of our marriage partner results in the increase of our love for him or her. Love not strengthened by the thought of death is shallow and changeable. We cannot fairly appreciate the value of life unless we think about the death of the person who is living.

I recommend to married people that they occasionally concentrate on every possible notion relating to their partner's death. This is not to prepare ourselves to live someday independent of our partner but to live together as closely as we can; that is, consider each other's life and death and thus live as an inseparable unit. In married life, each partner's independence isn't a highly admirable virtue, for it can be easily attained where there is contempt and unconcern between partners.

By meditating on our partner's death, we probably regret most not giving enough effort to making our partner happy and to causing less suffering. Think about our partner's reasonable wish, hope, and dream that couldn't be attained. Think about our partner's reasonable pain, agony, and gloom caused directly or indirectly by living married life. How much did we satisfy our partner and how much make our partner unnecessarily cry? A large part of married love arises when we recognize how incapable we are of making our partner happy, especially how

incapable we are of controlling our ego, for most of the misery we cause our partner could be avoided by controlling our ego.

To think and speculate about concrete moments of our partner's death by disease, accident, murder, suicide, etc., helps us to think about life. We may think various things about life, its frailty, brevity, unknown future, beauty, . . . but finally we will arrive at the conclusion that we have to live with more friendship and more help to each other. Marriage partners have the chance to live in this way and to know each other very deeply. Mutual help is the essence of married love.

In our meditation, imagine in detail about our partner's passing away. The rooms of the house, the outdoors, all will lose their color without the being of our partner. The clothes left in the closet, books, tools, kitchen utensils. . . . Recall the expressions on our partner's face on different occasions, tones of voice, gestures, the places visited together once and the places never visited, our partner with other people, friends, family, officials, etc. Then free ourselves from our meditation on our partner's death and live together again with our partner; that is the profoundness of married life.

What I have written does not present, I am sure, any unique and new knowledge or wisdom for our married life, and I do not believe there is a special medicine or theory helpful for married love. I think that for married life people have no need to concern themselves with fashion or newness at all, but it is important that each couple actually experience their own life of love. Their own love never comes from outside, it comes only from within their life. One hour's meditation on the death of one's partner is more helpful for married life than studying a hundred books.

Advancement of Married Love

Once we marry we believe and hope that joyful, substantial, and high married love will last forever and, moreover, increase. We even have the noble wish that our married love will influence other people in good ways. We think in this way because we dislike and fear to see our marriage break up. And sooner or later in our married life we become aware that our married happiness depends on the conscious advancement of our own married love.

But is it possible for our married love to advance infinitely? Isn't it the nature of things to wear out and ruin, and for married love also, from its highest peak around the time of our marriage ceremony, to gradually begin to decline? These fainthearted suspicions reasonably arise from seeing examples around us of marriages that didn't work out well, in which presumably married love didn't grow but diminished, faded, and rotted. Suspicions arise also from seeing our own occasional discouragements and crises, or the inactive, monotonous stagnation of love, even at its best, day after day.

Whether or not it is possible to advance married love should be judged by each individual couple from their own experience, for each case involves a different situation and personalities. Nevertheless, the essential virtues that enable us to advance our married love are what we can call wisdom and effort. There is the wisdom to distinguish which elements of our married love can grow and which elements can't. And there is the wisdom to recognize the deficiencies or imperfections in our married love, which make advancement difficult, and how to overcome them. Finally, there is the wisdom to be aware of obstacles and invaders that might endanger our married love, and how to avoid them.

Even though it takes effort to make ourselves follow whatever way our wisdom reveals to us, and even if it causes us some discomfort or suffering, still we have to do our best to put our wisdom into practice. In any case, our wisdom only shows us the way to protect our total life, and without our effort our wisdom can't make even a single flower grow.

No one can keep his or her physical youth, and therefore married love assisted by it has to yield to the love coming from our spiritual growth. No one can keep the enjoyment that comes from the excitement of newness at the beginning of marriage. So our enjoyment has to come from a continuous deepening of our everyday married love. The valued qualities that accompany us when we marry, such as our ability, knowledge, good nature, beauty, fortune, and position, will begin to lose their charm because our marriage partner is unable to appreciate them freshly and they begin to belong to the past. So the necessity of gaining newly cultivated valued qualities becomes more urgent in keeping our married love alive from present to future, instead of our looking back and clinging to the past. This sort of realization is the function of the first of the three kinds of wisdom I described above.

The second type of wisdom is not difficult to grasp properly if we are modest and honest with ourselves. We have to realize that our married love in the early stage of our married life is not perfect, strong, and steady, even if it seems to us that there is nothing to complain of and that we are in the happiest, most blessed moments then. In reality, what our early married love consists of is, rather, misunderstanding, no understanding, and wishful thinking, more or less. Naturally such an early married love is fragile and uncertain, and it needs a lot of protection and care, like a newly started seedling.

To recognize our imperfections and deficiencies is unpleasant, but it gives us the possibility of advancing our married love. Therefore we would do better to think more about

what things or acts of ours are preventing our partner's enjoyment than to think about what is giving our partner satisfaction.

With the third kind of wisdom we should know that the

obstacles and invaders that endanger our married love come from inside our marriage and are as bad as those coming from outside. Any crevice between marriage partners is an easy, inviting entrance for obstacles and invaders. Any crevice between a married couple and the society they live in also has to be regarded as an unprotected gate exposing their marriage to danger. A crevice between marriage partners originates when one partner runs on alone in an excessive pursuit of individual interest, leaving the other partner behind. Similarly a crevice opens between a married couple and society when the couple goes on alone and ignores society. Coexistence and mutual help, which is friendship, shouldn't be forgotten but should be the first rule in any situation. Common interest, being a centrifugal force to create peace, should come before any individual interest.

All three basic kinds of wisdom must be reexamined over and over again and must be carefully investigated by each couple. We have to recognize what are our own colorful, concrete problems. Recognizing what our problems are is the beginning of the advancement of our married love, for as long as there are problems we have to solve them. The process of solving is where our effort must be concentrated, and this process itself is the substance of advancing married love.

If we see from inside our married life, the substance of advancing married love is keeping morality. Our wisdom tells us what we should and shouldn't do to advance our married love. To practice what our wisdom tells us takes, for the most part, great effort, which means, keeping morality. However, it is clear that this morality isn't given or imposed from outside our marriage. We give it to ourselves, for our sake, for our enjoyment, to live by as we advance our married love. The substance of advancing married love is, therefore, to keep the morality we have made together. Whether we call it "morality," "rule," or "contract," we will realize that without it there is no advancement of our married love.

Married love that doesn't advance is fated to ruin, to germinate all sorts of poisonous bacteria. Marriage partners are not strongly bonded as if by a permanent glue, so sometimes they must think of themselves in the situation where each would be lonely again and whip themselves on to develop new ability. . . !

Freedom and Married Life

Some people think that marriage makes us unfree and that married life is a life of bondage. In marriage, one's individual interests must be submitted, they think, to a partner's approval, more or less, and various troublesome things will be demanded by the partner as a matter of course. More, they think that unwelcome responsibility follows after every action, and as time passes a married person can never be himself or herself, but will be forced to adjust to living under the constant watch of a partner, behaving so as to suit the partner's nerves. Thus, the thought of marrying is like the thought of putting oneself in a cage at the bottom of a shady valley where there is no chance for one's individual ability to develop or be exercised, no sunlight and no open space. With such a thought, some people may wish not to marry, or they may regret their commitment to marriage.

Certainly married life makes us unfree as individuals in some respects and no one has enough evidence to oppose or deny this fact. However, we have to study what freedom is for us and what its importance is before we decide to abandon the right to the merit of marriage. Everything has at least two faces, like the under and upper sides of a leaf. Naturally we can observe many faces of freedom, as many as there are adjectives. And definitions of freedom are so numerous that almost everyone has his or her own. This is because freedom is not only something given to us but also something we must realize by ourselves individually. It is possible for a prisoner to feel free even if he is greatly controlled in all of his physical conditions and circumstances. A ruling queen may feel unfree.

Freedom isn't always attained by being free of outside obstacles, but to attain freedom we absolutely need to recognize our own free being. Freedom can be defined as our recognition of our own inner free being. So, to attain freedom means to recognize our own free being, which isn't influenced by anything outside of us. To recognize our free being, we have to be pure, in a state in which we don't make any dualistic value judgments. We, with our utterly neutral self, face our own free being, that is, we become free being itself.

But existing as free being itself is almost the same as death. So as long as we live, we can't exist like that, or at least can't stay there extensively. This means that most of the time we can't make use of our free being in its true sense and can't live in freedom, even though we can for the moment recognize our free being and live a very limited, short period in freedom. We can only glimpse our freedom and believe there is such a state in which we are able to live in freedom. We therefore almost never see a person who lives with his or her freedom in this world. Instead we see mostly phony guys who try to give the impression that they are living in this way, or teachers who talk, talk, preach, preach, and educate us to seek freedom with their chaotic, drunken, pitiful confidence and shameless ignorance.

So what is important for us is not to grasp freedom but to live well or better in unfreedom. "Yes, we are unfree, and willing to live in unfreedom" is the realization we like to hear from people. "Freedom itself doesn't charm me. What creates joy in my life is the way of life in which I devote myself to training:

how much can I express my own individuality, how well can I become better and better, how deeply and how highly can I use the energy I possess to do worthy work in this unfree and suffering world?"

For the person who understands freedom and its importance in this way, the unfreedom accompanying married life isn't the sort of unfreedom that has to be disliked and avoided or feared. The unfreedom, bondage, duty, responsibility, trouble, pain, anxieties, etc., that occur in married life are, rather, welcome matters. They are often effective antidotes to one's evil free

enterprise. For the person who thinks that living his or her best in unfreedom is much more important than seeking freedom itself, there is naturally a distinction between good freedom and bad freedom. The question of how to live best in unfreedom, with the concern of clarifying what best is, spontaneously raises the question of what good and bad freedom are. So on the one hand, the bad freedom that charms a person in married life will be discouraged by the merit of the marriage partner. And on the other hand, those unfreedoms emanating from one's married life are most likely nice priming powder for one's good attempts. Unfreedom in married life serves to detach us from all evil allurements and to greatly encourage our good true nature. Any actions and their results that are not approved of or are discouraged by our married life are mostly useless or harmful in this human world. People are wise to hope not to attain bad freedom, which can be attained only by such conduct.

"The problem is," some may say, "there is useful and meaningful work in the world that can't be performed because of the unfreedom of marriage." In such a case, one has to choose either the merit of freedom or the merit of marriage. And if a person is so sure that a certain work will be restricted by marriage, why should he or she bother to marry in the first place? It would be better to live well with his or her honorable work without marrying, not creating any dishonorable misfortune for a partner by marriage. The wish for two contradictory merits even though, as I have said, they mostly don't conflict at all, is a very unsuitable dream for the person who is going to do great work for people.

The unfreedom of marriage is sweet, thankful, and pleasurable, the unmistakable fruit of life with one's beloved partner. In such an unfree life, why don't we do in the following correct order first, what we ought to do, second, what we can do, and third, what we want to do?

Unusual Marriages

When people care less about the appearance of their marriage and rather give greater value to its spiritual contents, the number of unusual couples tends to increase. The judgment of usual and unusual comes mostly from people's observation of form, and their observation often doesn't reach anything of substance. When it does, it proves that even the usual marriage can have unusual insights. A society not kind enough to care about spirituality puts most people into an old mold and encourages few people to break out.

The varieties of unusual marriages are many. There are international or mixed-racial marriages, young people married to old, marriages where one partner can't enjoy sex, economically rich married to economically poor, and so on. In the present world, these marriages are unusual because of the great differences in the physical or cultural conditions of the partners, but what they have in common is that the partners are of opposite sexes. Far more unusual are marriages between persons of the same sex, so-called homosexuals or lesbians. Such marriages don't stem from the physiological reproductive urge of mankind, though the couple might wish they could bear their own children.

Yet it is possible for partners of the same sex to marry, because marriage isn't exclusively for forming a family with children. In essence marriage usually means the state and process in which a husband and wife conceive and raise their new generation, and the life of the couple is valued and directed according to this fundamental meaning of marriage. Naturally those who fail, slight, or terminate this function have less need to continue their married life unless they increasingly reinforce other meanings of marriage. In that respect, both the usual marriage and the unusual lesbian and homosexual marriages face a similar state in which they all must find other constructive meanings for their marriage.

Of course especially those couples who choose an unusual marriage must have been finding their own meaning of marriage and the meaning they have found isn't a matter for others to criticize. Other people must take care not to lose their dignity in a low, self-deluded curiosity to peep into the life of an unusual couple. What is optimistic and encouraging about unusual marriages for those who live usual married lives is that though these marriages lack the usual basic function of marriage, still the partners can enjoy their married relationship.

It is apparent that usual married couples have more to study from unusual couples than the other way around. In society such courageous, unusual married couples must be able to contribute to deepening and widening the meaning of marriage, not by propagandizing their unusual marriage form but by clearly showing the meaning of their unusual marriage. For them the form of marriage isn't more important than its substance. The substance of their marriage is based not on animal physiology but on highly developed human spirituality, which means, having much more concern for our present and future human society than for producing systematized, stereotyped people.

Their spirituality can be manifested in the cultivation of

their friendship. In the usual marriage, too, friendship is an important part of the substance of marriage. But for a usual married couple the importance and situation of friendship is different from what it is for an unusual married couple. First, for a usual married couple friendship isn't always absolutely necessary, whereas for an unusual married couple it is absolutely

necessary, all the time, to sustain their married relationship. Second, for the usual married couple, because friendship is nursed between opposite sexes there is a certain impossibility, or sexual barrier, which limits a complete understanding of one another. Third, for the usual married couple there is more or less always the medium of their children between them, whereas unusual partners have to face each other directly. Thus, friendship in an unusual marriage is by any means not the same as friendship in a usual one. The unusual married couple must earnestly cultivate a direct and detailed friendship, constantly, with their own responsibility, or their unusual married relationship will lose the meaning of its existence and will break.

What is the difference between the friendship of an unusual married couple and the friendship of normal life outside marriage, such as with classmates, playmates, fellow workers, and comrades? All these normal friendships are evidently not deep enough and total enough relationships for marriage. Normal friendship has no commitment to taking responsibility for the sufferings of a partner and has no complete share in the enjoyment of a partner. Therefore normal friendship may be very partial, may be interrupted if inconvenient, and lasts no longer than a partner benefits from it. Once two people marry, they have to vow to help each other throughout their life, and whether they prefer to or not, or practice or not, each has to see the influence of his or her life on his or her partner's life. Marriage is to unify two spiritual lives, to live the greater single harmonious life with every possible help from the two differing bodies.

How does the relationship between teacher and student compare with the unusual marriage relationship? There can be a close similarity in the sense that in both relationships there is some worthy aim. However, teacher and student remain in a one-way relationship most of the time; that is, the teacher continues to be the one to teach and the student to be the one to be taught. Marriage partners can be both teacher and student at once and their positions can alternate freely according to the nature of each situation. Moreover, teacher and student are greatly limited in their area of influence on each other, because the nature of their relationship is to concentrate on a few particular subjects, and their concern is study. Once in our history it seems there were more totally life-involving relationships between teacher and student, especially if they were engaged in religious training, and indeed there are many traces of homosexuality in monasteries. However, I believe no teacher nowadays is wise enough to be such a total guide for every aspect of a student's life and no student is foolish enough to devote all of his life to a certain teacher.

Thus partners in the unusual marriage have the possibility and advantage of developing their unique friendship, which is unlike other types of human relations. It is an exclusive cultivation of each partner's true nature in a fair and totally devoted relationship. The essence of their marriage is to train themselves to be truly worthy human beings and to train their ability to recognize their partner as a truly worthy human being.

However, if they fail to see this essential meaning of their marriage, their marriage will be no more than a temporary and secondary replacement of the usual marriage. If they don't appreciate the advantage of their unusual marriage, gained by sacrificing the advantage of the usual marriage, what is left for them to appreciate but a life in which they are unable to marry at all? The importance of the meaning of marriage is in direct proportion to the importance of the life of those who marry, so whether we have a usual marriage or an unusual one, we must be kind to ourselves and to our marriage partner, whose life is so greatly involved with ours.

Divorce

To divorce is to abandon the continuation of a life of marriage with one's partner. To abandon means to lose hope, and to give up the will to build a better married life, to give up the will to contribute to the partner's happiness and share its merit. And it means to give up all necessary effort to attain that happiness and merit. Divorce is naturally a regrettable matter if the persons involved are normal, because it calls off a marriage formed with mutual love, trust, and respect, made possible mostly by the partners' own choice. It is as if a farmer were to sow wheat and destroy the crop by his own hand before harvest. It is a reckless act, impossible to be performed by an awakened person. If there is enjoyment to be derived from divorce, it comes only from the success of escaping from an outrageous partner. It is the enjoyment of being able to escape from a hole into which one fell after digging, but such humble enjoyment will be laughed at as foolish and poor-spirited by one's more serious mind. Divorce is a shameful thing, no matter what.

Divorce shows clearly to the persons involved that they possessed the ability to marry but not the ability to maintain and develop a married life. To divorce can therefore be a great opportunity to study, to know oneself and others and, more, to know society. This is true for persons involved in divorce more than for persons who are going to marry, if only the former frankly see the cause and process of the matter and wish to make it useful for their future. With such a point of view, one must perform the ceremony of divorce more solemnly and grandly than the marriage ceremony. Ceremonies are symbolic of the rapid deepening of our spiritual life. If a divorcing couple have children, they must take a responsible attitude as parents because the ill-influence of their divorce ranges over the family and isn't confined to themselves. Among the sufferings of children, there is none worse than the marriage quarrel of their parents.

Divorce, though an unwelcome and regrettable matter, is an opportunity to form a large and new determination to make others and oneself happy thereafter, to have a hope for the future with the realization that the persons involved paid an expensive compensation in order to study. So one shouldn't be pulled into a damp, dark place of regret, but should coolly reflect on what needs reflection. The wonderful meaning of our life is to create numerous instances of good out of evil. It is possible for those who divorce to marry again and live a worthy and joyful married life if they correctly reflect on their former marriage and determine not to repeat the same mistake.

People who divorce stand in the most suitable position to know what to reflect on. However, there are cases in which the persons involved have great difficulty seeing themselves fairly and clearly, just as it is said that a person deep in the mountains cannot see the mountains. This is because we see, judge, and think of matters from the center of our own profit and interest. So the person who wishes to reflect must nullify his or her own self, stand in the situation of the partner for the time being, and see things with the partner's eyes.

The essays written in this small book must be comprehensible and useful for people who couldn't avoid the experience of divorce as well as for people who strongly wish to have an excellently great married life. Frankly, I hope these essays will be read by people who are going to marry, but I think they won't

be well understood by them. Real things happen to be made in such a way that they are hard to understand without some experience of failure, suffering, and misfortune. The person who is going to live sincerely must always approach the true meanings of things straightforwardly instead of stagnating in the arguments of correct or incorrect usage of punctuation marks, words, and phrases. There isn't time to indulge oneself in constructing buildings of toothpicks except for the guy who is outrageously blessed with the ability to consume life in vain.

Loyalty

In married life, it is of course important that a husband and wife be loyal to each other, but more important is that each of them be loyal to themselves. Basically, loyalty means to be loyal to oneself rather than to others. To be loyal to oneself is to keep one's own dignity secure, regardless of one's partner. Hence it can be said that the person who is not awakened to his or her own dignity may not find it possible to be loyal to others.

One's own dignity can be maintained by doing one's best all the time wherever one has to stand. In detail, one must first establish one's subjective self. This means one must make of oneself a great element within one's environment, and do so out of one's own will and determination. In other words, one has to kill all those parts of oneself that are unsuitable to one's circumstances and bring to life all one's suitable parts. Second, one must live with one's subjective self thus established. One changes one's subjective self in relation to changes in one's circumstances, just as one doesn't allow one's subjective self to change in unchanged circumstances. In short, one maintains a disciplined and clear leadership in any environment in which one is also included. Third, one has to recognize with certainty the changeless parts of the environment, including oneself. And one has to love, respect, and enjoy the changeless parts and live with them as well as die with them. To do so is to long for and to seek absolute being far beyond relative matters.

Marriage partners are better off making an effort in friendship together to realize the dignity of each of their lives. This dignity is abstract and absolute but is inherent in their concrete and relative lives. They cannot be loyal to each other without recognizing the dignity of their lives. If they are blind

about dignity and yet talk about loyalty in marriage, their talk will sink to the level of two powers fighting for advantage, or the exchanges between mere, humble obedience and sharp, obstinate domination. Loyalty understood on such a low, animal level will disappear into thin air as soon as one or the other partner becomes a mental patient or passes away. Loyalty based on each other's dignity increases love and increases the longing felt by the one when the other suffers a long disease or dies. Married life continues even after the death of a partner. What kind of loyal person will be deluded with the thought of remarriage after the death of his or her partner?

It is hoped that a husband and wife will understand each other from their skin to the marrow of their bones just as light melts into water, and that they will have no reason to talk about loyalty. In such an ideal married life, of course we respect the dignity of each other, but shouldn't we respect the lives of violets and dandelions, shouldn't we live with the love and the enjoyment of coexisting with the pebbles of a stream, the moss of the rocks?

To Study Oneself in Married Life

One's life is not perfected solely by obtaining a lifelong companion. Certainly a person can become friends with another more or less similar human being in a fairly physical and emotional life as, having shoulders, one wears clothes and, having a mouth, one eats food. And it is true that the enjoyment of a harmonious friendship occupies a really important position among the enjoyments of one's life. This is so, because to have friendship means to complement the needs of another person, to help, to work together, to understand and sympathize with each other's weary troubles, to soften each other's pain and even to free each other from suffering . . . in short, to protect oneself from loneliness.

However, a person is not without internal problems that can hardly be understood by his or her partner and that are quite impossible to solve just by marrying and living together. "Why was I born and what will happen after my death?" "What is my life and what is the relation between my life and the life of others?" "How should I live?" "Why am I thus being?" All these are deeply rooted questions requiring very personal solutions, that is, they become the problem "to know oneself." If one tends to forget to solve this problem day after day and avoids facing its core as a result of being married, then it must inevitably be said that marriage is a tool to make a person waste his or her life in a shallow, cheap, and drunken manner. Such a marriage doesn't deepen a person. Instead, it indefinitely postpones his or her season of studying the real problem, and in consequence makes him or her eternally lose the chance to experience the great enjoyment of solving the real problem.

If we take a step down from such severe self-searching, at least we must understand that if a person has lost interest in religious, philosophical, and artistic matters and has given up seeking them only to bury himself or herself in the concerns of practical and daily matters, then the inner light of such a person's life will fade and the dignity of that life will rarely appear. Such a life could be replaced by any other without difficulty. A prosaic life has to follow the laws of material things.

Even about daily and common matters, when we think them over quietly, we know one's pain should be felt only by oneself, one's thirst cannot be satisfied by another person's drinking, and one's motions must be made by no one but oneself. For each person there are countless problems that no one else can solve. Who has painful feelings and can cure them by hearing another recall his or her various experiences and nostalgic places accumulated since babyhood? Who is more able to understand and sympathize with the unspeakable acts committed by oneself? One's own parents, brothers, and sisters live only with oneself, not in the mind of anyone else. Isn't it rather selfish, spoiled, or outrageously irresponsible to expect that any of these private problems would bring comforting words from one's marriage partner? Needless to say, as much as possible one ought to care about one's partner and practice the life of taking suffering from and giving pleasure to him or her. But I should say that a person was made with a very easy nature if he or she expects his or her deep inner problems to be solved by a partner's care and love. A

person is a profound being, with a mind hard to measure. Therefore such care and love from one's marriage partner falls short like an arrow shot to the sun, however taut the string of the bow.

A man or a woman is born alone and is alone when he or she dies. No one can live for another this good life of studying well one's own mind and being loyal to the law of one's own mind. In this vast universe there is only one person who has the possibility of knowing perfectly his or her own life. That one is oneself. What a pity if one doesn't help oneself, for we each are mere dust in this terribly wide, dark, and mysterious universe.

It is better not to marry if in marriage one is going to forget to study oneself. "What on earth am I?" is the biggest concern of everyone's life. Asking in order to seek its answer is religious training. Married life is most meaningful while both husband and wife encourage each other to train themselves. Thus, training life and married life can be synonymous.

Then, how is one to solve one's own matters? There are a thousand ways, each different, and there is no particular way. In any case, one has to endeavor. A husband and wife are better off walking the same way together. A person who loses his or her way amid the mist would do better to meditate calmly even if he or she decreases attendance at church to once from ten times. Make his or her own altar even if its size is one thousandth of that of the church. Quietly meditate together, husband and wife, even if only ten minutes morning and evening. Then ask deeply to your very personal self, "What am I doing now, here?" "Why am I here like this?" and "Who am I?" If marriage partners love each other, they can help each other to do so and go on hand in hand.

"Then after that, what and how should we . . . ?" There is no reason to waste words on it, because people who train themselves will spontaneously understand when the time comes. Courageously, go straight on.

To Have Children

For most people, marriage and children are not necessarily one and the same thing, yet for most people, living a married life and having children are related in large and small ways and in fact the two are inseparable.

Now, this set of essays is for and about the married life of marriage partners, though I wish someday to write various matters about the problems of the relation between parents and children. I am only noting here the most necessary ways of thinking about children, and it is my hope that they will be recognized as such by parents or by those who will become parents.

For people who could fortunately come across a suitable partner with marriage as a result, it is a natural wish to have children with their united blood. The enjoyment of being able to marry ought to occupy a large part of their happiness in life. The person who knows the enjoyment of marriage knows the enjoyment of life. It is a matter of fact that the person who knows the enjoyment of life wishes to share it with others directly or indirectly. Wishing to have children has the same taste of enjoyment that one has from marriage, so one wishes to have one's children.

It is unlikely that people would wish to have children if they are suffering and understanding life as a continuation of pains from morning to night. For them, too, children will be born, but it is as one of their mistakes or as a consequence of momentary pleasure sought in order to escape a life of suffering. For such people there is no will to produce children and there is neither the enjoyment nor the consciousness of being parents. Their conduct in making children is a ghostly floatation, and they are unqualified human beings, in no way superior to beasts. Therefore it is wise for people not to make children if they are not yet experiencing the enjoyment of marriage and married life.

In the married life of each beloved partner, the highest enjoyment is found in the process of raising and nursing creatures hand in hand. If they are loving each other, they feel considerable enjoyment just by walking together along a path. Cleaning the house and taking care of a garden together makes them very happy. Even if together they have to face an enemy, even an ugly war, they are able to feel enjoyment. Much more so, to love and to raise, not to destroy, things, and to work together makes them truly happy. Everyone, if normal, wishes to do so. In short, a husband and wife who love each other want to have children, wish to give birth and to nurse.

In our present, so-called civilized society, the reasons for having children are these basic two: to share the enjoyment that the persons involved are having, and to cooperate with a beloved partner in working to bring up their children. Various other reasons, even though they differ according to the persons and their situation, nevertheless must in general be waved aside. For instance, a fairly noble reason, such as to produce children for the sake of the continuation of mankind, has very ambiguous meaning. Moreover, the prevailing point of view at present is that having children is not only unnecessary but in fact unwelcome unless either a third world war or a global epidemic occurs. Some may give more low-level reasons for having children, such as the hope that they will be taken care of in their old age by their children, or that their friends are cheerful with their own children, or to entrust their unperformed dream to their children. Such people act as if human beings happen to have neither the ability to think nor deep love and compassion and have only the selfish instinct to protect themselves. Certainly in them there is no beauty and no charm as human fellows.

Then, I hope that people who are going to have children with the right reasons won't forget, or don't need to remember, because of their well-digested comprehension, the following several principles:

1) Parents have a duty toward their children from beginning to end even though they haven't a bit of right. There are numerous necessities that parents have to provide for their children, which no substitute can provide, and this is the performance of their duty and not the practice of their right. It is fine if parents only exert themselves for their children, welcome suffering, do all they can, and at the same time hope for only the things that their children wish them to hope for. It is an evident truth that the ones who produced the children are their parents, regardless of whether it was right or wrong, and the children have no way to take responsibility for it.

2) Children aren't the possessions of their parents. Children merely appear at the place of so-called parents to be brought up temporarily, through the complicated as well as strange and mysterious law of cause and effect in the universe. Children have their independent humanity from the very beginning and yet they act like dependent creatures until they reach a mature age. In trying to make sense of this puzzling state, parents may think their children are like that because they are engaged in examining

the greatness of their parents and wishing to perfect it. And if parents think so, they will not totally misunderstand.

3) Children should be respected and should never be despised, because they are far better than most parents about purity, a great vitality to live, unlimited future possibility, etc. Parents who are unable to see the greatness of their children are fools who are unaware of their own foolishness. And parents

who scorn the inferiority and undeveloped abilities of their children are inebriates who have forgotten their own advancement. We must fear, just as we fear a fire, to take advantage of weak children and to attempt to make them obey for any selfish interest of ours. To reexamine, how many truly justifiable accusations are there among the things that children cannot escape being called, such as "spoiled," "ill-behaved," "egoistic," "naughty," "unreasonable," "conceited," "cowardly," and so on and on? Aren't there too many instances of such accusations rather fitting the parents themselves when we see each child as one individual with character and when we consider his or her total life instead of only parts of his or her life, on a universal scale?

4) Parents must be diligent to make good circumstances. They must hope to make a good person, then give at first a good environment. It can be easily understood that there is a suitable situation for producing a thief if we wish to produce a thief. No baby is born with the desire to be a thief in the future, but there are as many environments fitted to educating thieves as there are trash cans in this world.

It is difficult to determine what good is and what bad is. Even if we understand what good is, making a good environment is more difficult. No matter how much a family endeavors to make a good environment, unless the total society improves, the environment of the children can be harmful to them after all.

However, when I speak of a good and a bad environment, I mean the good commonly blessed by everyone and not the good that differs according to each individual opinion. That is to say, the peace of the world is good, and whoever works for it is a good person.

Or, truth is good, and whoever seeks it is a good person. I am not talking about such relative good as worldly success, skill in earning money, or attainment of a high education. Therefore my hope to parents is that they make a good environment in which their children can easily grow to be persons who will contribute to peace and will seek truth. Is it a good or a bad beginning for children who might possibly become ambassadors of peace to grow up amidst the quarrels of their parents? Are parents who leave things half done, who begrudge effort, who pursue pleasure, and who ridicule a sober life offering their children a place where they can grow to be earnest truth seekers? It is difficult to prepare a good environment, but it is to be hoped that children's parents will take pains to do so more than their parents did for them. Everyone, as long as they wish to live, seeks peace and truth.

5) Teach children thoroughly at an early age that people will die. This is a perfect law without a single exception in a million cases. To make a person's life valuable, we have to know the fact that a person dies. People who don't know it, who don't think about it, and who forget about it spend their lives in waste. Life is respectable and beautiful. When children realize that it is so, their lives begin to bloom. It is meaningless and sad that one must float and sink like a dream in this world without knowing what life is and what death is. To teach children about death is at once to teach the sorrow and fear of mankind. To teach these subjects to our beloved children is unbearable and a matter we wish to avoid — maybe they will become neurotic or psychopathic, and we rather hope to hold only birthday parties in our home.

However, not teaching about death is almost equal to not teaching about life. Then, we must ask ourselves: what kind of parents do our children hope to have? Do they hope to have parents who are able to teach not only about death and life but also about enjoyment, sorrow, fear, and composure? Most children, in my observation, don't have such parents but have parents who know very little about life, who are unwilling to think about death, and who in quick succession feel joy and sorrow about only shallow sensational matters. Isn't there any church or temple where one can obtain the Law of life and the universe? In church or temple is there no father or priest who teaches about that? In the districts where weeds have grown rank, are priests plucking fowls, or in air-conditioned rooms are they watching pro football on TV with Bible in hand? It couldn't be so; there must be some great ones somewhere, only they are too great to be easily distinguished.

These five principles, I think, are the general principles to which parents should give their concern, though there may be more. To marry and to have children as well is not easy, even though it may seem so. To live one's married life is certainly to train oneself. It doesn't matter at all whether we add a small 'rs' or only 's' after 'M.' If we spend our days washing the sands of the ocean, when are we going to clean our mind? My wife recently had occasion to write these poems:

> If to enjoy, you put your dear children aside,
> Please fear they will go out again
> Into the far and wide universe
> From which they come but once.

> For the selfish way
> there's a price to pay—
> It is higher than if
> you give all away.

About the Author

Seikan Hasegawa, born in a temple near Kyoto, Japan, in 1945, became a Buddhist priest at age fourteen. He studied Northern Buddhism in a Japanese Zen monastery and also studied Southern Buddhism in a Thai monastery. He first came to America in 1969. He is the author of two other books, *The Cave of Poison Grass: Essays on the Hannya Sutra* and *Mind to Mind.*